INSIDE THE NFL

HOUSTON TEXANS

by Charlie Beattie

Abdo & Daughters
MIDDLE GRADE NONFICTION

An imprint of Abdo Publishing
abdobooks.com

ABDOBOOKS.COM

Published by Abdo Publishing, a division of ABDO, PO Box 398166, Minneapolis, Minnesota 55439.

Printed in China.
052025
092025

THIS BOOK CONTAINS RECYCLED MATERIALS

Cover Photos: Luke Hales/Getty Images Sport/Getty Images (C. J. Stroud); Ronald C. Modra/Getty Images Sport/Getty Images (Andre Johnson)
Interior Photos: Cooper Neill/Getty Images Sport/Getty Images, 4-5, 11, 55, 63; Perry Knotts/Getty Images Sport/Getty Images, 6; Maria Lysaker/AP Images, 7; David Eulitt/Getty Images Sport/Getty Images, 8, 61 (bottom right); Leslie Plaza Johnson/Icon Sportswire/Getty Images, 9; Abdo Publishing, 12-13; George Gojkovich/Getty Images Sport/Getty Images, 14-15, 31, 60 (bottom right); Pat Sullivan/AP Images, 16, 60 (bottom left); Ronald Martinez/Getty Images Sport/Getty Images, 17, 18, 20; Ed Betz/AP Images, 21; Thomas B. Shea/Icon SMI 750/Newscom, 22; Brett Coomer/AP Images, 23; Scott Boehm/AP Images, 24-25, 60 (bottom middle); Robert E. Klein/AP Images, 26; Paul Spinelli/AP Images, 27; Bill Baptist/Getty Images Sport/Getty Images, 28; G. Newman Lowrance/AP Images, 29, 60 (top); Tony Gutierrez/AP Images, 30, 43, 61 (bottom left); Thomas B. Shea/Icon Sport Media/Icon Sportswire/Getty Images, 32; Thomas B. Shea/Getty Images Sport/Getty Images, 33; Dave Einsel/AP Images, 34-35, 45, 61 (top left); Bob Levey/Getty Images Sport/Getty Images, 36-37, 38, 52, 53, 61 (top right); Al Messerschmidt/Getty Images Sport/Getty Images, 39; Eric Gay/AP Images, 40; Smiley N. Pool/Houston Chronicle/AP Images, 41; Peter Aiken/Getty Images Sport/Getty Images, 44; Wesley Hitt/Getty Images Sport/Getty Images, 46; Maddie Meyer/Getty Images Sport/Getty Images, 47; Jonathan Ferrey/Getty Images Sport/Getty Images, 48-49; Tim Warner/Getty Images Sport/Getty Images, 50; Jeffrey Brown/Icon Sportswire/Getty Images, 51; Ken Murray/Icon Sportswire/Getty Images, 54, 59; Carmen Mandato/Getty Images Sport/Getty Images, 57; Shutterstock Images, 58

Editor: Haley Williams
Series Designer: Laura Graphenteen
Production Designer: Ryan Gale

Library of Congress Control Number: 2024948499

Publisher's Cataloging-in-Publication Data

Names: Beattie, Charlie, author.
Title: Houston Texans / by Charlie Beattie
Description: Minneapolis, Minnesota: Abdo Publishing, 2026 | Series: Inside the NFL | Includes online resources and index.
Identifiers: ISBN 9781098296742 (lib. bdg.) | ISBN 9798384919261 (ebook)
Subjects: LCSH: Houston Texans (Football team)--Juvenile literature. | National Football League--Juvenile literature. | Football teams--Juvenile literature. | American football--Juvenile literature.
Classification: DDC 796.333--dc23

CONTENTS

Houston Texans quarterback C. J. Stroud looks for a receiver against the Tampa Bay Buccaneers in November 2023.

CHAPTER 1

STROUD'S BIG DAY

THE HOUSTON TEXANS TOOK THE FIELD TRAILING BY FOUR WITH 46 seconds to go. The Tampa Bay Buccaneers had just scored a go-ahead touchdown to silence the crowd at NRG Stadium in Houston. But the Buccaneers had left a sliver of time on the clock, and the confident rookie quarterback C. J. Stroud wasn't worried. "Give me the ball," Stroud later said about his thoughts in the moment. "Call the plays. I'm going to make the plays."

When the Texans took the field against the Buccaneers on November 5, 2023, they faced a make-or-break game. After an 0–2 start to the season, Houston had won three of its next five games. The Texans were 3–4 going into the Week 9 game against Tampa Bay.

Stroud was a big reason for the turnaround. The quarterback had started to turn heads

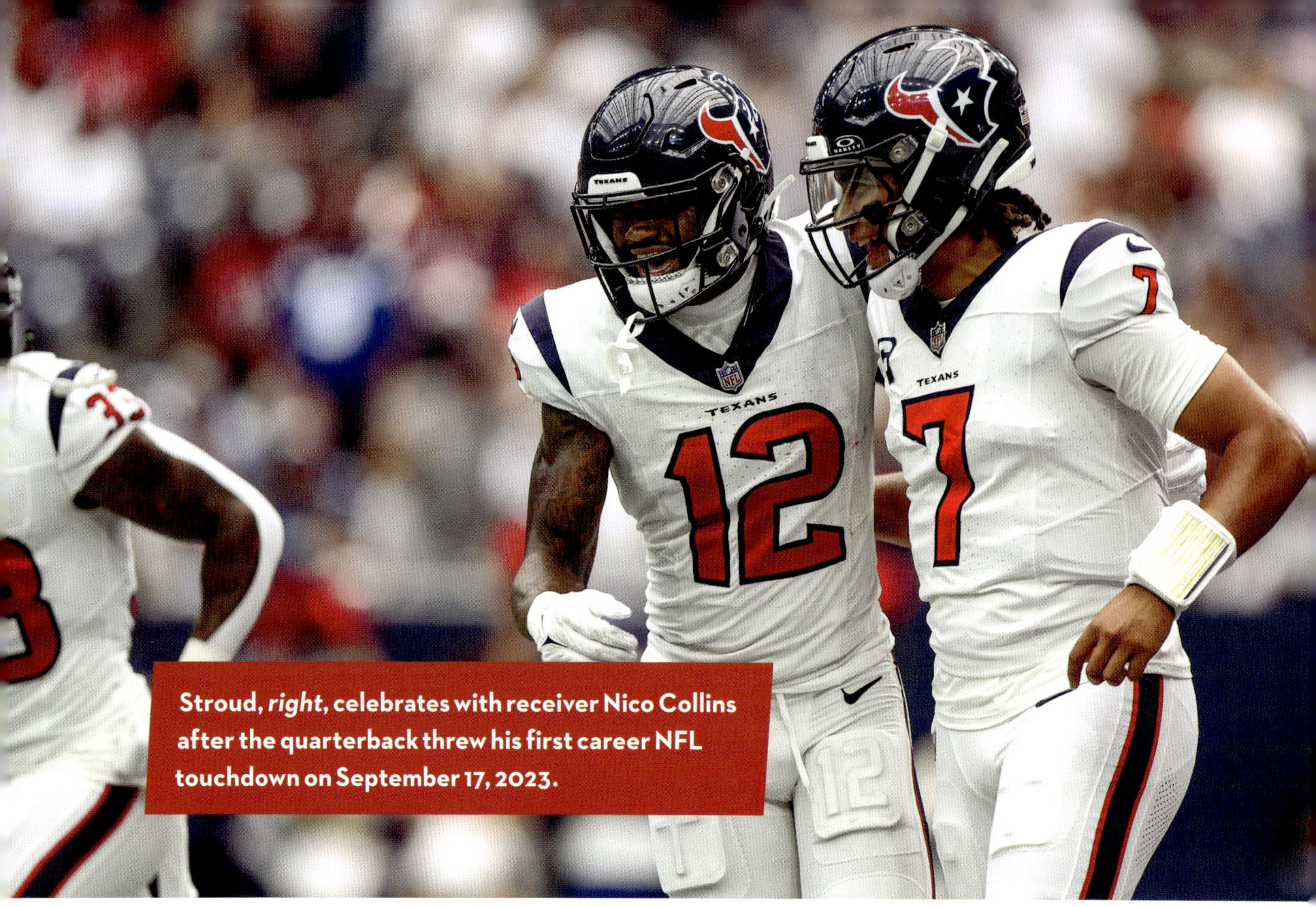

Stroud, *right*, celebrates with receiver Nico Collins after the quarterback threw his first career NFL touchdown on September 17, 2023.

around the National Football League (NFL). Through his first seven games, the rookie from Ohio State had thrown nine touchdowns and only one interception. During that stretch, he also celebrated his 22nd birthday, making him one of the youngest players in the league.

HOPE ARRIVES

NFL teams rarely thrive without a good quarterback. Houston had been looking for one for years as the team entered the 2023 draft. The previous three seasons, the Texans had been one of the NFL's worst teams. In that stretch, they compiled a record of 11-38-1.

Before the 2023 season, the team hired a new head coach, DeMeco Ryans. One of his first tasks was to find a new quarterback.

Luckily, there were several good options in the upcoming draft, and the Texans held the second pick.

Stroud was one of the top prospects. In two years as the starter at Ohio State, Stroud had posted eye-popping numbers. In 2021, he had thrown for more than 4,400 yards and 44 touchdowns. A year later, he tossed 41 scores.

When the draft began, the Texans wasted no time in snapping up Stroud. They just needed to get him ready for the rigors of the NFL. That's where Ryans came in. The former NFL star linebacker put the rookie through tough practices in training camp. Ryans made sure Stroud could handle NFL blitzes by pressuring the quarterback relentlessly. Stroud adapted quickly and won the starting job when the 2023 season opened.

A YOUNG ACTIVIST

In 2015, when C. J. Stroud was just 13 years old, his father was sentenced to 38 years in prison. As Stroud got older, he became very interested in prison reform. The young quarterback has done extensive work advocating for better living conditions in prison facilities. He even showed his support for the cause. During a 2023 game, Stroud wore shoes that read "#REFORM" as part of the NFL's "My Cause My Cleats" initiative.

A HOT START

Stroud didn't throw a touchdown pass in his first game. However, he still impressed people in the 25-9 loss to the Baltimore Ravens after throwing for 242 yards. The next week, Stroud completed 30 of 47 passes for 384 yards and threw two touchdowns in a 31–20 loss to the Indianapolis Colts. A week later, he added two more scores and 280 yards. That made him just the third NFL quarterback to throw for more than 900 yards in his first three games. Even better, that performance earned Stroud his first NFL win, a 37–17 romp over Houston's division rival, the Jacksonville Jaguars.

Although the wins came and went, Stroud's performances stayed strong. But the week before the Tampa Bay game, he struggled in an ugly loss to the previously winless Carolina Panthers. Now it

Stroud poses with NFL commissioner Roger Goodell at the 2023 draft.

was time for Stroud to show another side of his character. He would need to prove that he could bounce back on a big stage.

RECORD BREAKER

When a rookie quarterback struggles after a handful of good games, NFL observers start to wonder whether the league has figured him out. Stroud took the field against the Buccaneers knowing he would need to wipe away those doubts. Early in the game, he offered up the perfect response. On Houston's second drive, Stroud completed four passes for 58 yards. His final toss was a 14-yard touchdown to receiver Nico Collins to put the Texans up 7–3.

Collins (12) caught seven touchdown passes from Stroud (7) in 2023, the most of any Texans receiver that season.

Stroud was just getting started. He opened the third quarter by tossing a 75-yard touchdown to receiver Noah Brown. Stroud then added two more touchdown passes, one to fellow rookie Tank Dell and one to tight end

Dalton Schultz. However, the Buccaneers offense had matched Stroud blow for blow all game. And with 46 seconds left, Tampa Bay quarterback Baker Mayfield threw a 14-yard touchdown pass to put the Buccaneers up 37–33.

Only four NFL rookie quarterbacks had ever thrown five touchdown passes in a game. To win this game, Stroud would have to match that feat. The young quarterback completed a pair of passes, with the Texans calling timeouts after each one to stop the clock. After Stroud threw another pass to get his team to the Tampa Bay 41-yard line, he spiked the ball to stop the clock again.

Just 16 seconds remained. That left Houston time for only a few plays. On the next snap, Stroud lofted a pass to Dell for 26 yards along the left sideline. Dell stepped out of bounds with 10 seconds on the clock.

As Stroud scanned the field on the next play, he spotted Dell racing across the middle of the end zone. Stroud showed off his arm strength as he lasered a pass between two defenders. Dell reached out and snagged the ball, then pulled it close as he landed in the end zone for the winning score. "That drive—man it was special," Stroud said after the game.

"THAT DRIVE—MAN IT WAS SPECIAL."

—C. J. STROUD

The 39–37 victory was amazing enough. However, Stroud's final numbers were staggering. He threw for an NFL rookie record of 470 yards. And his five touchdown passes matched the rookie record. The Texans improved to 4–4, and they owed it all to a rising young star.

Stroud's 470 passing yards against Tampa Bay were the most by a Texans quarterback in 11 years.

NFL TEAMS MAP

NFC

NFC EAST

- DALLAS COWBOYS
- NEW YORK GIANTS
- PHILADELPHIA EAGLES
- WASHINGTON COMMANDERS

NFC WEST

- ARIZONA CARDINALS
- LOS ANGELES RAMS
- SAN FRANCISCO 49ERS
- SEATTLE SEAHAWKS

NFC NORTH

- CHICAGO BEARS
- DETROIT LIONS
- GREEN BAY PACKERS
- MINNESOTA VIKINGS

NFC SOUTH

- ATLANTA FALCONS
- CAROLINA PANTHERS
- NEW ORLEANS SAINTS
- TAMPA BAY BUCCANEERS

AFC

AFC EAST

- BUFFALO BILLS
- MIAMI DOLPHINS
- NEW ENGLAND PATRIOTS
- NEW YORK JETS

AFC WEST

- DENVER BRONCOS
- KANSAS CITY CHIEFS
- LAS VEGAS RAIDERS
- LOS ANGELES CHARGERS

AFC NORTH

- BALTIMORE RAVENS
- CINCINNATI BENGALS
- CLEVELAND BROWNS
- PITTSBURGH STEELERS

AFC SOUTH

- HOUSTON TEXANS
- INDIANAPOLIS COLTS
- JACKSONVILLE JAGUARS
- TENNESSEE TITANS

The Oilers played in Houston from 1960 to 1996.

CHAPTER 2

HOUSTON'S NEW TEAM

In 1997, billionaire Bob McNair was looking to bring a National Hockey League (NHL) team to his hometown of Houston. McNair thought he had a strong case. Houston was one of the largest cities in the United States, boasting a big media presence. It also had a history of successful minor league hockey.

However, the NHL turned McNair's bid down in June of that year. Although he was disappointed, McNair quickly saw an opportunity to create a team for a different sport. Earlier that year, Houston's longtime professional football team, the Oilers, moved to Nashville, Tennessee, and became the Titans. The Oilers had been in Houston since 1960, when they joined the American Football League (AFL). That league merged with the NFL in 1970.

Despite their rich history in Texas, the Oilers had grown unhappy in Houston. After years of fighting with the city over a new stadium, Oilers owner Bud Adams became fed up and moved the team. Ironically, Nashville was also one of the cities that beat out McNair's bid for an NHL expansion team. But McNair quickly spotted a new quest. Instead of hockey, he could bring Texas's favorite sport back.

A THREE-HORSE RACE

The NFL was looking to expand from 30 teams to 32 in the late 1990s. One of the new spots was already claimed. The Cleveland Browns, who had moved to Baltimore and become the Ravens in 1995, were returning as a new team in 1999. But the 32nd team

Although Bob McNair was born in Florida, he had called Houston home since 1960.

The construction of Reliant Stadium, later renamed NRG Stadium, was a major factor in the NFL's consideration of Houston's expansion bid.

was set to join the league in 2002. Houston certainly had a strong case, as a huge city in a football-mad state that had recently lost a popular team. However, McNair's bid faced a strong competitor.

Los Angeles, the nation's second-largest city, didn't have an NFL team either. Not only was it bigger than Houston, but it was also one of the media capitals of the United States. Furthermore, Los Angeles had recently lost not one but two teams. In the mid-1990s, the Raiders had moved to Oakland, and the Rams went to St. Louis.

So it was no surprise that in 1999, the other 31 NFL owners voted 29–2 to add Los Angeles to the league, leaving Houston out. But soon after, cracks started to appear in the Los Angeles owners' bid. Two competing ownership groups were fighting over the team, and the city was unwilling to help either build a new stadium.

By October 1999, the other owners had seen enough. And when McNair's $700 million bid topped Los Angeles's by $150 million, the NFL took the higher offer. Houston would have its new team in 2002. Not only that, but the city would also have a gleaming new retractable-roof stadium. As part of the deal, the Super Bowl would be held in Houston in February 2004.

BUILDING A TEAM

McNair got right to work putting together a football operation. He hired Charley Casserly to run the team. As Washington's general manager, Casserly had helped build three championship teams in the 1980s and early 1990s. Then McNair got to work on a namc for the team.

The nickname "Oilers" was not an option since that belonged to the former Houston team. But McNair put in the paperwork to trademark a host of new options. The three finalists were Apollos, Stallions, and Texans. Not wanting to add another horse-themed nickname to the NFL, which already had the Denver Broncos and the Indianapolis Colts, McNair went with Texans.

The Texans' mascot is a bull named Toro.

"The Texan name is distinctive," McNair said. "When people around the country hear Texans, they're going to know immediately that it's Houston's NFL team."

> ***"WHEN PEOPLE AROUND THE COUNTRY HEAR TEXANS, THEY'RE GOING TO KNOW IMMEDIATELY THAT IT'S HOUSTON'S NFL TEAM."***
>
> ***—BOB MCNAIR***

The nickname had some history in Texas. In 1952, an NFL team called the Dallas Texans played one season in the league. The team finished 1–11 and quickly folded. Then, in 1960, a different Dallas Texans team was formed. These Texans were one of the Oilers' AFL rivals. The two teams even met in the league's championship game in 1962. A year later, the AFL's Texans moved to Kansas City, Missouri, and became the Chiefs.

COACHES AND PLAYERS

Now it was Casserly's job to fill out a roster and a coaching staff. He chose respected head coach Dom Capers to lead the Texans. Capers had a history with expansion teams, having brought the Carolina Panthers into the NFL in 1995. They reached the National Football Conference (NFC) title game one year later.

Building a full roster took Houston more than a year. The team signed a handful of free agents in December 2001. Two months later, the Texans took part in an expansion draft. The team could either select between 30 and 42 players from other teams or pick players whose contracts added up to $28 million. Because some of the Texans' picks were more expensive, the team drafted only 19 players. But Houston thought it had some potential stars. Linebacker Jamie Sharper had won a Super Bowl as a key member of the Baltimore Ravens just two years earlier. Defensive tackle

Gary Walker was a stout run defender who started his career with the Houston Oilers in 1995. Veteran cornerback Aaron Glenn was a two-time Pro Bowl pick coming off a five-interception season for the New York Jets in 2001.

However, Houston's top priority was getting Tony Boselli. The mammoth left tackle had been one of the best at his position since joining the NFL with the Jacksonville Jaguars in 1995. He made the Pro Bowl every year from 1996 through 2000. But in 2001, he was limited to three games by a shoulder injury that required surgery. Jacksonville left Boselli available for the expansion draft, and Houston grabbed him with the first pick.

The Texans were hoping left tackle Tony Boselli would be an essential part of their offense when they picked him first in the expansion draft.

The Texans needed someone such as Boselli to protect the player they wanted to pick with the top selection in the 2002 NFL Draft. The prize was quarterback David Carr out of Fresno State.

David Carr, *center*, was considered the top prospect in the 2002 NFL Draft.

The Texans grabbed Carr, hoping he would be the star quarterback they needed.

TAKING THE FIELD

By the time Houston was ready to play an official game, its shiny new home was complete. Reliant Stadium was the first retractable-roof dome in the NFL's history. On the notoriously hot early-season days, the roof could be closed to keep fans cool. That was the case when the in-state rival Dallas Cowboys arrived in Houston on September 8, 2002, for the season opener. The Texans were considered a huge underdog. But in front of more than 69,000 fans and a national television audience, Houston rolled to a 19–10 victory.

Linebacker Jay Foreman, *left*, tackles Dallas Cowboys running back Emmitt Smith in Houston's 2002 season opener.

The win wasn't pretty, though. Carr completed only 10 of 22 passes. But he drew a roar from the crowd just 1:14 into the game when he connected with tight end Billy Miller for the Texans' first touchdown. The noise was still deafening with 12:18 to go in the game when Carr threw a 65-yard touchdown to receiver Corey Bradford to break a 10–10 tie. As the final seconds ticked down, the crowd chanted "Thank You, Bob" to McNair for making pro football possible again in Houston.

With that, Houston became the first expansion team in 41 years to win its opening game. However, it was not a sign of things to come. The offense failed to score a touchdown in either of the next two games, and the Texans lost five straight. The team limped to a

4-12 record behind an offense that averaged a league-worst 13.3 points per game.

One of the biggest reasons for Houston's offensive struggles was its blocking. The team had been counting on Boselli to anchor the offensive line. But an injury meant he didn't play a single down for the Texans. Without protection, Carr was pummeled all season. The rookie was sacked 76 times to set an NFL record. As he ran for his life, Carr threw only nine touchdown passes against 15 interceptions. He also fumbled 21 times, with seven recovered by opponents.

DEFENSIVE STANDOUTS

Although the Texans struggled on offense in their first season, the defense was a pleasant surprise. Defensive tackle Gary Walker and cornerback Aaron Glenn each made the Pro Bowl that year. Only once before had an expansion team fielded multiple Pro Bowl picks in its first season.

The fact that Houston won four games was a testament to its defense. Late in the season, the defensive unit helped the Texans pull out one of the strangest wins in NFL history. On December 8, 2002, Houston traveled to Pittsburgh to face the playoff-bound Steelers. Houston won 24–6 thanks to three defensive touchdowns. Glenn had interception scores of 65 and 70 yards. The blowout win helped mask the fact that Houston's offense had gained only 47 yards all day. That was the lowest total by a winning team in NFL history.

Aaron Glenn was one of the Texans' best defensive players in their early seasons.

During his career with the Texans, wide receiver Andre Johnson (80) caught 1,012 passes, including 64 touchdowns.

CHAPTER 3

IN THE WILDERNESS

HOUSTON STARTED ITS SECOND SEASON BY GIVING DAVID CARR A NEW weapon at receiver. The Texans selected towering wide receiver Andre Johnson with their top pick in the 2003 draft. Instantly, he became one of Houston's most important stars. The quiet and steady Johnson would spend 12 years with the team, making highlight-reel catches on his way to the Pro Football Hall of Fame.

Johnson caught 66 passes as a rookie, giving fans a taste of what was to come. However, that was about all that went right for Houston that season. Although Carr was sacked only 15 times, he threw just nine touchdown passes compared to 13 interceptions. His backup, Tony Banks, won two games to Carr's three, despite Banks only making three starts. Houston finished 5-11.

Quarterback David Carr, *right*, is sacked in a 2006 game against the New England Patriots.

A BIG DECISION

The next two seasons weren't much better. Carr was battered in every game. In both years, the Texans' signal-caller was sacked more than any other quarterback in the NFL. Carr stood in and took the pounding bravely, never missing a game. But at the end of the 2005 season, the Texans had the NFL's worst record at 2–14. Along with that, many people thought Carr was a bust.

With the top pick in the 2006 draft, Houston had an opportunity to reset. The two biggest names in college football were in contention for the top selection. Running back Reggie Bush had been the face of a dominant University of Southern California (USC) program. In 2005, he led the Trojans to the national championship game. In a classic encounter, USC was beaten by another top prospect, quarterback Vince Young of Texas.

Both Bush and Young were electrifying. The slender Bush's highlight-reel runs featured crafty spins, shifty jukes, and blazing speed. Young, at 6 feet, 5 inches and 232 pounds with speed, was a phenom of a quarterback. When he wasn't launching deep throws to speedy receivers, he could easily beat a team by running the ball.

Running back Domanick Davis, also known as Domanick Williams, rushed for more than 1,000 yards in 2003 and 2004. He had almost 980 yards in 2005 before an injury ended his career.

Everyone assumed the Texans would take one of the two players. However, when draft night rolled around, Houston shocked the football world when the team selected defensive end Mario Williams

Houston fans boo at a draft party after the Texans select Mario Williams as the top pick in 2006.

from North Carolina State. While Williams was good, the thought of leaving potential game changers on the board infuriated Texans fans, who booed the choice. Afterward, Casserly defended Williams at a press conference, saying, "If somebody doesn't like it, then I'm right here, and I'm the guy to yell at. . . . Boo me. Don't boo Mario Williams."

> ***"IF SOMEBODY DOESN'T LIKE IT, THEN I'M RIGHT HERE, AND I'M THE GUY TO YELL AT. . . . BOO ME. DON'T BOO MARIO WILLIAMS."***
>
> ***—CHARLEY CASSERLY***

It didn't help that Bush spent his rookie season just across the border from Texas in New Orleans. There, he flashed his skills by scoring on the ground, through the air, and in the return game. Young went third to Houston's division rival, the Tennessee Titans. In his first year, he beat Houston twice on his way to being named the

Despite a rocky start with Houston fans, defensive end Mario Williams spent six seasons with the Texans and made the Pro Bowl twice.

NFL's Offensive Rookie of the Year. Young added insult to injury with a game-winning 39-yard touchdown in overtime in the second meeting. Although Williams sacked Young in the teams' first matchup, it was one of only 4 1/2 he amassed all year.

While Houston fans didn't love their first pick, they came to adore the team's second-rounder. Linebacker DeMeco Ryans was an instant star. He led the NFL in solo tackles as a rookie and was named the league's Defensive Rookie of the Year.

PUTTING IT TOGETHER

Additions such as Ryans helped Houston slowly climb out of the cellar. In the team's first six years, the Texans finished last in the American Football Conference (AFC) South five times. But Ryans became the leader of an improving defense. Even Williams became a standout player, totaling 14 sacks in his second season.

Linebacker DeMeco Ryans, *left*, had a team-high 156 tackles in 2006.

On offense, the Texans had Johnson as well as young tight end Owen Daniels as stellar pass catchers. But after another poor season in 2006, it became clear that Carr was not the player to get them the ball. After the season, the Texans let him go and brought in quarterback Matt Schaub from the Atlanta Falcons.

Houston also had a smart offensive mind in new head coach Gary Kubiak, who was brought in during the 2006 season. A former backup quarterback to the legendary John Elway on the Denver Broncos, Kubiak was thought of as a coach who could get the best out of Schaub. However, while Schaub was an improvement over Carr, he struggled to stay on the field, missing five games in each of his first two seasons with the Texans.

Finally, in 2009, Schaub stayed healthy, and the results followed. The former third-round pick led the NFL with 4,770 passing yards while throwing 29 touchdowns. His most dependable target was once again Johnson. The All-Pro player led the league in receiving

Matt Schaub was one of the top statistical quarterbacks during his time with the Texans, but injuries often kept him off the field.

Fans high-five Texans players after the team defeated the New England Patriots on the last day of the 2009 season.

yards for the second straight season, racking up 1,569. He also caught nine touchdowns.

Despite enduring four straight losses to start the second half of the season, the Texans mustered a late winning streak. On the final day of the season, the playoffs were within reach, but Houston needed to beat the powerhouse New England Patriots. The Texans were behind 27-13 early in the fourth quarter before rallying. Schaub connected with receiver Jacoby Jones with just over nine minutes left, and two rushing touchdowns from undrafted rookie running back Arian Foster secured the win. However, the Texans' joy did not last long. Later that day, the New York Jets won their game. Despite a 9-7 record that marked the Texans' first winning season, they missed the playoffs in the competitive AFC.

STAR BACK

Schaub was a reliable quarterback for Houston. Johnson was perhaps the top pass catcher in the NFL. The dependable Ryans was the leader of an improving Texans defense. And Williams reached the Pro Bowl in both 2008 and 2009. However, the team had never had a consistent star running back. In 2010, Houston found one in an unlikely place.

As a college senior at Tennessee in 2008, Foster struggled. Once thought of as a good NFL prospect, he rushed for only 570 yards and one touchdown. After no teams picked Foster in the 2009 draft, the Texans signed him as a free agent. Foster worked his way into a starting role by the end of the year. His two touchdowns against the Patriots in Week 17 showed fans he could be a go-to back.

DEEP STEEL THUNDER

Fans at Houston games have long been entertained by a pep band. Originally called the Bull Pen Pep Band, it first played at a draft party in 2002. The band was eventually renamed Deep Steel Thunder. In 2024, the horns section was removed from the band, leaving only a drumline.

There are 36 members of Deep Steel Thunder.

Foster cemented his position as a starter in Week 1 of the 2010 season. Facing the division-rival Indianapolis Colts, the second-year back exploded. He rushed for a team-record 231 yards in a 34–24 win. For the rest of the year, Foster proved his big game wasn't a fluke. He led the NFL with 1,616 rushing yards and 18 total touchdowns, 16 of those rushing.

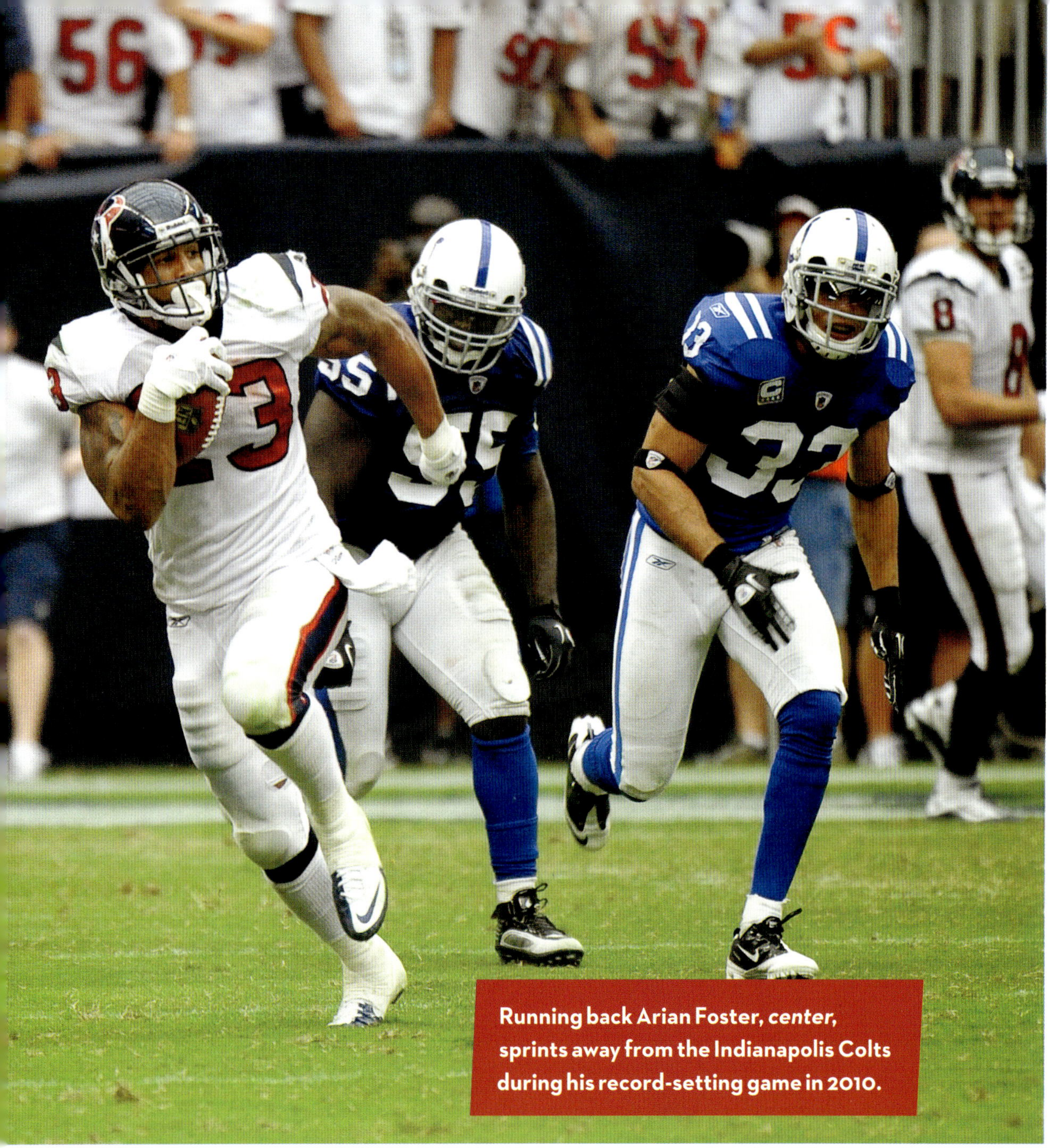

Running back Arian Foster, *center*, sprints away from the Indianapolis Colts during his record-setting game in 2010.

Houston rolled to a 4–2 start, but the team struggled down the stretch. The Texans lost eight of their next nine games, many in excruciating fashion. Five of those losses came by a touchdown or less. The 6–10 season looked like a slide in the standings. But for a team that needed more help to become a contender, it was just what Houston needed in the long run.

Defensive coordinator Wade Phillips helped turn Houston into one of the NFL's toughest defensive teams.

CHAPTER 4

SUCCESS AT LAST

THE 2010 HOUSTON TEXANS FEATURED A STRONG OFFENSE. However, their defense was one of the worst in the NFL. To fix that problem, the team hired a coach whose name was familiar to Houston football fans.

In the 1970s, Bum Phillips was the head coach of the Houston Oilers. The quotable, cowboy hat-wearing coach led the team to some of its finest seasons, including a couple of AFC title game appearances. By 2011, Bum had long retired. But his son, Wade Phillips, was carrying on the family tradition of football coaching. The younger Phillips was considered one of the best defensive minds in the NFL. Before the 2011 season, Houston coach Gary Kubiak hired Phillips as his defensive coordinator.

Linebacker Brian Cushing, *left*, was known as one of the hardest hitters in the NFL during his time with the Texans.

Phillips had talent to work with. DeMeco Ryans was returning after missing all but six games the year before. He was joined at inside linebacker by the hard-nosed Brian Cushing. The pair were a good fit for Phillips's preferred 3–4 defensive system, which needed two strong tacklers in the middle. To help along the defensive line, the Texans drafted J. J. Watt, an imposing defensive end from Wisconsin. Meanwhile, free agent cornerback Johnathan Joseph anchored the secondary.

A PAINFUL TITLE

The Texans entered the 2011 season ready to compete on both sides of the ball. The defense had allowed the third-most yards in the league in 2010. In their first year under Phillips, they improved to allow the second fewest. Although Andre Johnson was limited by injuries, Arian Foster rushed for more than 1,200 yards and 10 touchdowns. Houston rolled to a 7–3 start.

Cornerback Johnathan Joseph, *right*, intercepted 17 passes in nine years with the Texans. Four of those were returned for touchdowns.

Those wins came at a heavy cost, though. In a 37–9 romp over the Tampa Bay Buccaneers in Week 10, Matt Schaub injured his foot. The starting quarterback was out for the season. In his place came Matt Leinart, a

Arian Foster (23) rushed for more than 6,400 yards in seven seasons with the Texans.

former college star who had been signed in the offseason. Leinart lasted less than one week before he was knocked out with a broken collarbone in a game against the Jacksonville Jaguars.

That left the Texans with untested third-string quarterback T. J. Yates. The rookie from North Carolina had thrown just 15 passes that season, which all came during the Week 11 win against the Jaguars. But he held his own in a 17–10 win over the Atlanta Falcons the following week. With a 9–3 record, Houston was one win away from clinching its first division title, and with it a playoff appearance.

Facing the Cincinnati Bengals, the Texans fell behind 16–3 at halftime. Houston then clawed back in the second half. With 2:33 to play, Yates and the offense took over at Houston's 20-yard line, trailing 19–13. Yates went to work, slowly moving the team down the field. But with under one minute to play, the Bengals sacked him for a 5-yard loss. That set up third-and-15 at the Bengals' 40. Yates dropped back and was immediately pressured again. This time, he scrambled, eluded a tackle, and banged off another tackler for a 17-yard pickup to keep the drive alive.

Five plays later, the Texans had second-and-goal at the Cincinnati 6-yard line. With only eight seconds on the clock, Yates dropped back and fired a bullet to receiver Kevin Walter in the

Receiver Kevin Walter (83) catches the game-winning touchdown against the Cincinnati Bengals in 2011 to clinch the Texans' first playoff appearance.

end zone. Kicker Neil Rackers added the extra point to seal the 20–19 comeback win and a division title.

J. J.'S DAY

The Texans lost their last three games of the 2011 season. That set up another matchup with the Bengals in the wild-card round of the playoffs. Both teams started rookie quarterbacks, which had never happened in the playoffs before. However, a rookie defensive player was the one who stole the show and announced himself as a star in the making.

Watt had been inconsistent during his first year, recording only 5 1/2 sacks. At times, Houston fans booed him. But he saved his biggest moment for the postseason. With the game tied 10–10 and under a minute left in the first half, Bengals quarterback Andy Dalton tried to throw a pass to the right side of the field. Watt, while being blocked by a Bengals player, leaped to bat the ball down. Instead, the pass stuck in his hands. With an open field in front of him, Watt raced 31 yards to the end zone, crossed the goal line, and then raised the ball high in salute to the crowd at Reliant Stadium. He held tight to the ball as teammates mobbed him on his way to the sideline.

Watt's score was the key play in a 31–10 win for the Texans. Houston was not only a playoff team, but a playoff winner. Watt continued his strong performance in the next round against the Baltimore Ravens, finishing the game with 2 1/2 sacks. However, Yates struggled against the excellent Ravens defense. His three interceptions doomed the Texans to a 20–13 defeat.

Defensive end J. J. Watt celebrates his pick six in the playoff game against the Bengals after the 2011 season.

RECORD SETTERS

Behind Watt, Houston entered 2012 as a favored pick to reach the Super Bowl. And he was as good as promised. Through Houston's season-opening five-game winning streak, Watt piled up 7 1/2 sacks. That was just the start of a season in which he recorded 20 1/2 sacks, four forced fumbles, two recoveries, and 16 deflected passes.

Rarely had one player had such an effect on NFL games defensively. Phillips said of Watt's play, "He had the best season ever. Nobody's ever had a season like that." At the end of the year, Watt was an easy choice as the NFL's Defensive Player of the Year.

"[WATT] HAD THE BEST SEASON EVER. NOBODY'S EVER HAD A SEASON LIKE THAT."

—WADE PHILLIPS

Watt's sacks were easily a team record. But he wasn't the only Houston player to find his way into NFL history books in 2012. Schaub and Johnson

Watt's 101 career sacks for the Texans were almost twice as many as the next-highest Houston player when he left the team in 2021.

were fully healthy again. In a Week 11 game against the Jaguars, they fired their way into football lore.

The Texans entered the game 8–1. Jacksonville was a lowly 1–8. However, the game turned into a shootout. That suited Houston's quarterback and star receiver just fine. On the team's opening drive, Schaub and Johnson connected on three consecutive plays, totaling 74 yards.

The teams were back and forth all game, and eventually needed overtime. With just over two minutes left in the extra period, the game remained tied 37–37. On second-and-five, Schaub flipped a quick screen pass to Johnson. Following a pair of blockers, the star receiver sprinted 48 yards for the winning score.

Andre Johnson (80) leaps into the crowd to celebrate his game-winning touchdown against the Jacksonville Jaguars in 2012.

It was Johnson's first touchdown of the day. His 14 receptions during the game were a team record, and his 273 receiving yards were the most by an NFL player in 12 years. Schaub ended the day with 527 passing yards, tied for the second-most in NFL history. The game-winning touchdown pass was his fifth of the day.

COMING UP SHORT

The Texans won the AFC South again in 2012 with a record of 12–4. After squeaking past the Bengals 19–13 in the wild-card round, Houston faced the New England Patriots. Despite 343 passing yards from Schaub and a two-touchdown game for Foster, the Texans fell 41–28.

Houston started the 2013 season 2–0, but then everything went wrong. The Texans lost their final 14 games. That proved to be the end of the road for several of the team's key pieces. Kubiak was fired with three games left. Schaub, who had been injured during the season and struggled when he was on the field, was traded at the end of the year.

Head coach Bill O'Brien, *left*, talks to Tom Savage, one of the many quarterbacks the Texans started during the mid-2010s.

Finding a consistent quarterback is an ongoing challenge for NFL teams. And after Schaub left, Houston struggled to find a fit. Between 2013 and 2015, seven players started at quarterback for the Texans. New coach Bill O'Brien's team still managed to win a division title in 2015 thanks to a strong defense led by Watt, who was again named Defensive Player of the Year. But after a wild-card loss in which journeyman Brian Hoyer threw four interceptions, the team entered 2016 looking for a star quarterback.

To fix the problem, Houston signed quarterback Brock Osweiler. The year before, Osweiler had won five games filling in for injured legend Peyton Manning on the Denver Broncos. In the offseason, the Texans committed $72 million over four years in hopes that Osweiler was the answer.

BULLS ON PARADE

The Texans' playoff seasons in the 2010s came with a blistering soundtrack. The team fired up the crowd by playing the 1996 song "Bulls on Parade" by Rage Against the Machine. The Texans connected the song to their logo, which features the Texas state flag inside a bull's head.

Instead, it turned into an expensive mistake. Although Houston finished 9-7 and won the AFC South, Osweiler threw 15 touchdowns and 16 interceptions. The team managed to win another home playoff game, beating the undermanned Oakland Raiders in the wild-card round. But the Patriots picked off Osweiler three times in a Texans loss the following week. After that year, the Texans traded Osweiler to the Cleveland Browns. Then, Houston went looking for a new quarterback to lead the offense.

Quarterback Brock Osweiler (17) is sacked in the divisional playoff game between the Texans and the New England Patriots on January 14, 2017.

The Texans selected quarterback Deshaun Watson with the 12th pick in the 2017 NFL Draft.

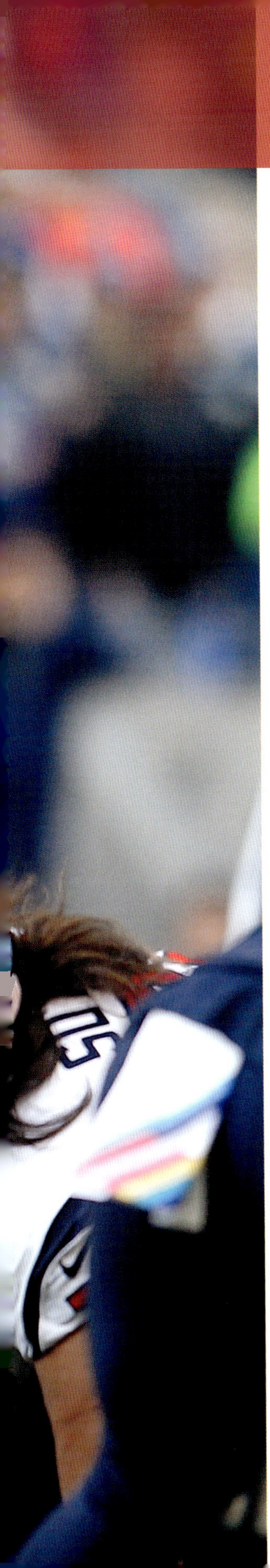

CHAPTER 5

SIGNAL-CALLERS

THE TEXANS ENTERED WEEK 4 OF THE 2017 SEASON WITH A MODEST 1–2 record. But there was reason for optimism. The Texans had selected quarterback Deshaun Watson in the first round of that year's draft. In college, Watson had led Clemson to a national title. Then, in Week 3 of his rookie season, Watson held his own against the mighty New England Patriots, throwing two touchdown passes. Although Houston fell just short, losing 36–33, the young quarterback had shown a lot of promise.

As the Tennessee Titans entered the now-renamed NRG Stadium in Houston for Week 4, a buzz was building about Watson. And he got to work early against the Titans. He threw an 8-yard touchdown pass to Pro Bowl receiver DeAndre Hopkins late in the first quarter.

Wide receiver Will Fuller (15) hauls in a touchdown during Houston's rout of the Tennessee Titans in 2017.

After Watson hit receiver Will Fuller on a 16-yard toss early in the second, Houston had a 21–0 lead. By the time Watson plunged in from 1 yard out with 1:19 left in the half, Houston led 30–14.

The day was far from over for Watson. He threw two more touchdown passes in the second half, and Houston rolled to a 57–14 victory. The rookie's incredible day featured 283 passing yards, another 24 rushing, and five total touchdowns. It was a signal that a star had arrived for the Texans. However, the hype was delayed four weeks later when Watson injured his knee in practice and was lost for the season. Even so, there was hope in Houston.

THE STREAK

Watson recovered in time for the 2018 season. So did J. J. Watt, who had played only eight games in two years due to various injuries. However, even with their star players back on the field, the Texans lost their first three games of the season, all by a touchdown or less.

Houston appeared headed for a tie in Week 4 against the Indianapolis Colts. But kicker Ka'imi Fairbairn saved the day by knocking in a game-winning 37-yard field goal as time expired in overtime. Fairbairn was the hero again the following week against the Dallas Cowboys, booting a 36-yard winner with 1:50 left in overtime.

Those exciting finishes were just the beginning. Behind strong play from Watson and a 16-sack season from Watt, the Texans reeled off a team-record nine consecutive wins. During the streak, Watson showed just how tough he was. The quarterback broke his ribs

Kicker Ka'imi Fairbairn (7) boots the game-winning field goal in overtime in the first 2018 matchup between the Texans and Indianapolis Colts.

and injured a lung in a Week 6 win over the Buffalo Bills. The injury made flying on a plane impossible, since the air pressure change could do more damage. Instead of missing time, Watson took a 12-hour bus ride to Jacksonville the next week, then threw for 139 yards and a touchdown in a 20–7 win over the Jaguars.

Despite the strong season from Watson, Houston couldn't get over its playoff hurdles. The Texans hosted the Colts in the wild-card round. The Indianapolis defense sacked Watson three times, dominating in a 21–7 win over the Texans.

BOB MCNAIR'S CHARITY WORK

Bob McNair was well-known for his charitable contributions during his time as the Texans' owner. After Hurricane Harvey devastated Houston in 2017, McNair and his wife, Janice, donated $3 million to relief causes. The hurricane forced a Texans preseason game to be moved to Arlington, Texas. The McNairs donated the amount of money the game would have made in ticket sales and concessions to also help the relief efforts.

Bob McNair

THE SPIN

By the end of the 2019 season, there was little doubt that Watson was an emerging NFL star. He led Houston to a 10–6 record and a home playoff game against the Buffalo Bills. The matchup was billed as Watson against Josh Allen, Buffalo's budding star at quarterback.

In reality, both players spent the game running for their lives. The Texans sacked Allen three times, forcing him to fumble twice. Watson had

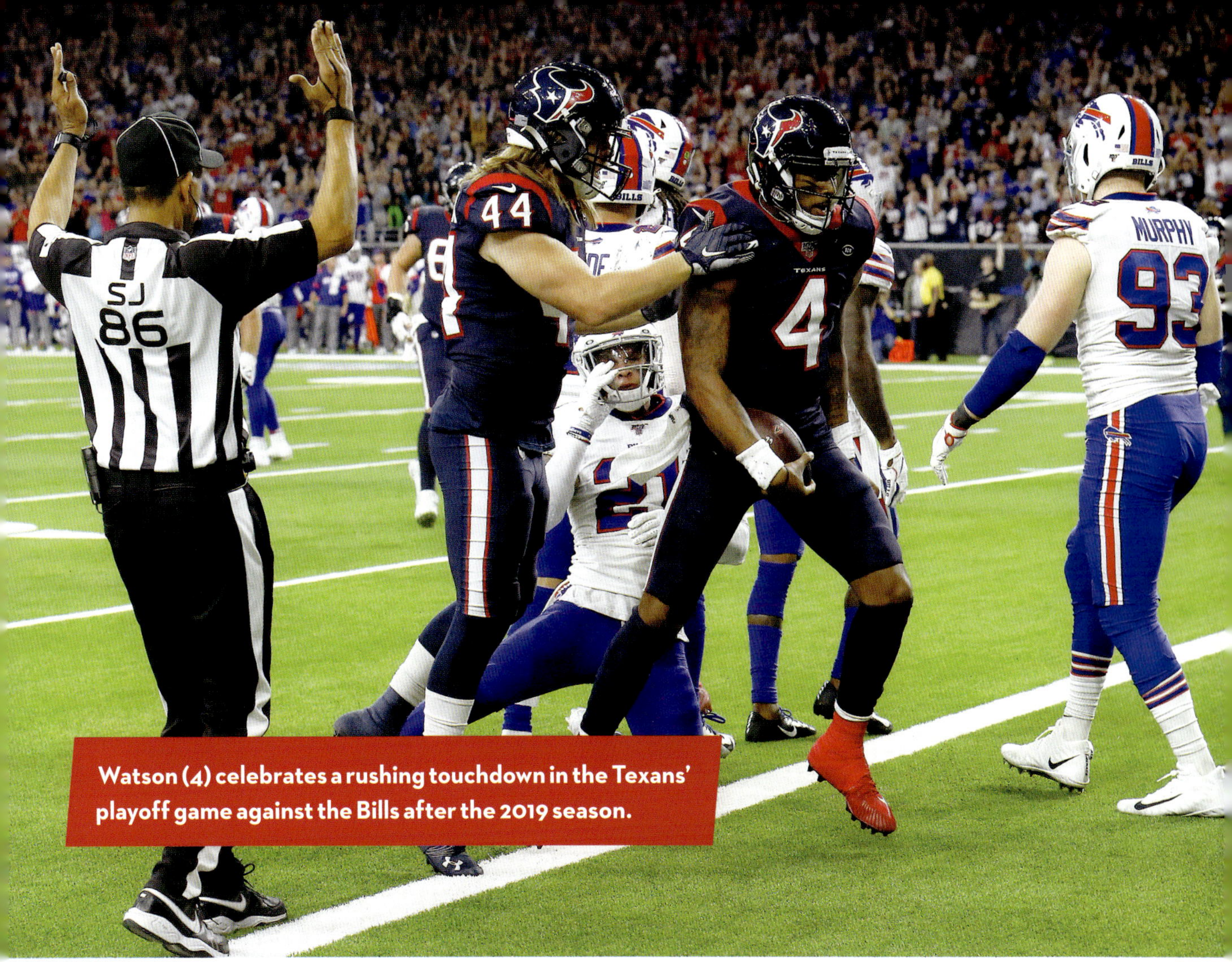

Watson (4) celebrates a rushing touchdown in the Texans' playoff game against the Bills after the 2019 season.

it even worse, as he was sacked seven times that game. Late in the third quarter, Buffalo built a 16–0 lead against Houston.

Once again showing his toughness, Watson shook off the hits and mounted a comeback. Late in the third, he scrambled 20 yards for a touchdown, and a two-point conversion made it 16–8. Watson then led two scoring drives in the fourth quarter. After a field goal on the first, he hit running back Carlos Hyde on a 5-yard touchdown pass for a 19–16 lead.

However, the Bills tied the game on a late field goal, sending it into overtime. Both teams failed to score on their first drives of the extra session. Houston then took over at its own 19. Watson slowly guided the Texans down the field. With 4:16 left, they faced second-and-six at the Buffalo 44.

As Watson dropped back to pass, two Buffalo defenders attacked on a blitz. With a defender on either side, Watson had nowhere to go. But instead of taking an eighth sack, Watson spun away. The two blitzers collided, and Watson scrambled away to his right. He then threw a short pass to running back Taiwan Jones, who raced to the Buffalo 10-yard line. On the next play, Fairbairn kicked a game-winning 28-yard field goal.

Running back Carlos Hyde crosses the goal line for a touchdown during the playoff game between the Texans and Buffalo Bills after the 2019 season.

The win sent the Texans on the road to Kansas City for the divisional round. In all of Houston's playoff appearances, the team had yet to win a postseason game on the road. That streak appeared to be coming to an end in the second quarter. Behind two touchdown passes by

J. J. Watt leaves the field after Houston's overtime playoff victory against the Bills.

Watson, a field goal, and a blocked punt for a score, Houston raced to a 24–0 lead against the heavily favored Chiefs with 10:54 left in the second quarter.

After that, though, everything went wrong. Kansas City scored a touchdown to cut into the lead. Then, upon being stopped on the next drive, Houston coach Bill O'Brien curiously called for a fake punt from inside the Texans' own 35. It didn't work, and Kansas City quickly scored again. By halftime, the lead was gone, and the Chiefs never looked back. Houston allowed 41 straight points and eventually lost 51–31. Houston's playoff road losing streak continued.

STARTING OVER

The defeat against the Chiefs should have been a temporary setback for a talented Houston team. Instead, it was the start of a disastrous stretch. The Texans traded Hopkins, their best receiver, just weeks after the loss to Kansas City. The move blindsided fans. But the receiver and his head coach didn't get along and could no longer work together. Without Hopkins, Houston stumbled to a 4–12 record in 2020. O'Brien was fired, and Watt left the team as a free agent in early 2021.

In March 2021, a female massage therapist filed a lawsuit against Watson alleging inappropriate behavior. In the coming months, 25 more women came forward to accuse him. The news shocked fans. As the team's quarterback, Watson was also the Texans' public face. For his first few years in the NFL, Watson had seemingly been a positive influence on both the team and the city. Suddenly, that all came crashing down.

As the lawsuits played out, Watson sat out the 2021 campaign. Although he eventually was not charged with any crimes, Watson became an NFL outcast. Houston traded him to the Cleveland Browns in 2022.

The situation surrounding Watson contributed to a feeling of instability within the team. Frequent coaching changes didn't help. After O'Brien, David Culley led Houston for one year in 2021. The team then hired former Chicago Bears coach Lovie Smith. He, too, lasted only one unsuccessful season. As had been the case throughout much of Houston's history, neither coach had a reliable quarterback to lean on.

Entering the 2023 season, Houston sought to fix both its coaching and quarterback problems. For their coach, the team brought back former star linebacker DeMeco Ryans. After retiring in 2016, Ryans had built a successful career as an assistant with the San Francisco 49ers, including helping the team reach a Super Bowl as a position coach.

Then, in the 2023 draft, the Texans appeared to strike gold by selecting C. J. Stroud with the second pick. Stroud became just the fifth rookie to throw for more than 4,000 yards in a season. His stellar play led the Texans back to the playoffs. In the second quarter of the wild-card round against the Cleveland Browns, Stroud threw 37- and 76-yard touchdown passes. That helped Houston build a 24–14 halftime lead. The defense put it away in the second half. Cornerback Steven Nelson and linebacker Christian Harris each

Wide receiver Brandin Cooks caught 147 passes and nine touchdowns across the 2021 and 2022 seasons.

TEXANS TROPHY CASE

SUPER BOWL CHAMPIONSHIPS: 0

DIVISION TITLES: 8

AFC South: 2011, 2012, 2015, 2016, 2018, 2019, 2023, 2024

All stats are through the 2024 season.

returned an interception for a touchdown as the Texans rolled to a 45–14 victory.

Once again, that win was at home. But even Stroud's presence couldn't help Houston earn a road playoff victory. The Texans lost 34–10 to the Ravens in Baltimore the next week. Still, at just 22 years old, Stroud had already become the youngest quarterback to ever win a postseason game.

In 2024, the Texans defended their AFC South title. While Stroud led the offense, young stars such as cornerback Derek Stingley Jr. and defensive end Will Anderson Jr. anchored a stout defense. In the wild-card round of the playoffs, the Texans started slow at home against the Los Angeles Chargers. Late in the second quarter,

C. J. Stroud looks to pass in the playoff game between the Texans and Los Angeles Chargers in January 2025.

Stroud connected with Nico Collins for a touchdown to give Houston a 7-6 lead. From there, the Texans rolled. Stingley Jr. intercepted two passes, while Anderson Jr. racked up 1 1/2 sacks to seal the 32–12 win.

The following week, Houston's issues in road playoff games struck again in the divisional round. The two-time defending Super Bowl champion Kansas City Chiefs sacked Stroud eight times. Houston lost 23–14. Despite another early end in the playoffs, the Texans had plenty of young talent to build around for years to come.

TIMELINE

Bob McNair's $700 million bid for an expansion team is approved by the NFL.
1999

2000
Houston's new team announces its nickname as the "Texans."

The Texans win their first game 19–10 over the Dallas Cowboys.
2002

2003
The Texans select wide receiver Andre Johnson as their top draft pick.

Houston chooses defensive end Mario Williams with the first pick in the draft.
2006

2007
Houston trades for quarterback Matt Schaub to replace David Carr.

The Texans finish with their first winning record but just miss a playoff spot.
2009

Running back Arian Foster leads the NFL with 1,616 rushing yards.

2010

2012

J. J. Watt's pick six against the Cincinnati Bengals on January 7 seals Houston's first playoff win.

2015

Watt wins the Defensive Player of the Year Award for the third time in four seasons.

Quarterback Deshaun Watson leads the Texans to a playoff win over the Buffalo Bills on January 4.

2019

2023

Quarterback C. J. Stroud sets an NFL rookie record with 470 passing yards in a game against the Tampa Bay Buccaneers.

GLOSSARY

blitz–when a linebacker or defensive back attacks the line of scrimmage to stop a run or sack the quarterback.

bust–a player or team that was expected to do well but fails to succeed.

contender–a person or team that has a good chance at winning a championship.

coordinator–an assistant coach who is in charge of the offense, defense, or special teams.

draft–a system that allows teams to acquire new players coming into the league.

expansion team–a new team that is added to an existing league.

fluke–an unlikely event that occurs thanks to a stroke of luck.

fumble–losing the ball and allowing the opponent a chance to recover it.

journeyman–a player who has played for many teams or has been unable to find a specific role.

merge–join with another to create something new, such as a company, a team, or a league.

outcast–a person who is cast out by society.

Pro Bowl–a postseason competition that the NFL's all-stars are invited to compete in.

reform–positive change.

retractable–able to be opened or closed.

rival–an opponent with whom a player or team has a fierce and ongoing competition.

rookie–a professional athlete in his or her first year of competition.

sack–a tackle of the quarterback behind the line of scrimmage before he can pass the ball.

training camp–a set of practices held before the season to prepare for competition.

underdog–the person or team that is not expected to win.

veteran–someone who has played for many years.

ONLINE RESOURCES

Booklinks NONFICTION NETWORK
FREE! ONLINE NONFICTION RESOURCES

To learn more about the Houston Texans, please visit **abdobooklinks.com** or scan this QR code. These links are routinely monitored and updated to provide the most current information available.

INDEX